Upon the Page

Deborah L. Kelly

ISBN: 978-1-989940-14-3
© 2020 Deborah L. Kelly
Dimensionfold Publishing

Contents

Upon the Page 1
Fire of Passion 2
Spirit'Song 3
Child of the Universe 4
Daydream 5
Paper & the Word: A Love Story 6
Everything Ends 7
I … 8
Cotton Candy Boat 9
Violet Petals 10
A Mother's Hands 11
As Old As I Used to Be 12
Through the Veil You Walk 13
A Million Shining Hearts 15
The Unseen Lands of Here and There 16
Christmas Eve Musings: 2020 17
Crystal Fire 19
Clay of the Earth 20
A Million Stars 21
This Great Lady 22
Essence 23
Moondust 24
Step for Step 25

Within the Crystal	26
Language of Music	27
Wings Upon Angels	28
Kindred to the Magpie	30
White Lion	32
Star Traveller	33
A Brighter Day	34
A Kelly Warrior	35
A Note To Behçet's	37
A Pittance from Few	39
Akashic Connection	41
The Hippie	42

Upon the Page

I write the words upon the page
of modern times and ancient age.
Of dreams come true, and angel's wings;
trees so green, and birds that sing.

Of love and hope; dreams come true;
this, my friend, I offer you.
May inspiration flow through your door;
deliver you to distant shores.

Shores of mystery, wonder; intrigue.
This place, which no one else has seen.
Rolling waves and salty air;
breeze blowing softly through my hair.

I write the words upon the page;
myrrh and lavender, rose and sage.
Candles, crystals, cloth and seams;
magic *always* accompanies dreams.

Spin the wheel of silken toil;
'naught to take; the wealth of spoil.
Threads from spindle twist and spin;
brings out beauty locked within.

Now, with tapestry complete;
of golden thread, and proper seed
planted within the silken threads;
a story of ancients, those who once led.

Fire of Passion

His wings spread as he sees his
reflection mirrored in the beautiful
waters of lapus lazuli. Covered
in radiant golden glow of autumn dress;
she shines on him, as talons flare
to grasp that which we do not see.

Crown of white; eyes to facilitate
piercing mortal soul with memories
of the ages; sages call to him
in the whisper of ether in which
he flies. Proud, majestic wings
of freedom spread outwards
to the four corners of the earth.
Path ever ascendant; heart
noble and strong; a rhapsody
plays within the chords of his
breast. Standing the test of corporeal
flight, the night in its velvet offers
solace as he searches for the fire;
sparking wings to lift him higher.
Fire of passion; fire of dreams;
let it burn deep into you as you
fly with this great master.
On a quiet night, you can see forever
from his wing.

Galaxies sing in the wide
open spaces of endless flight.

Spirit'Song

Spirit'song of wild, blue embers
glowing through December's
cold fires of snow.

Spirit'song of river running
in tune to light orbs
of living matter.

Spirit'song of mountain forest
flowing with a chorus
of smooth, soft loam.

Spirit'song of sky above
gives us rainbows of
etheric love.

Spirit'song, morning bright;
there is no darkness in our night,
for all is bright and luminous here.

Spirit'song take me along your
flowing shores; let me rest upon
tomorrow's arrival of bliss.

Spirit'song lend me an ear
that I may sing along with the music
of eternal and compassionate soul.

Flowing whole through mountain dreams;
all the seams are sewn with diamonds.

Child of the Universe

This child of the universe dreams
of a better, brighter world.
She stands, motionless, as the cosmos
swirls and dances around her.
Within the heart of every child
we find innocence, true Faith;
a healing view of life and all it holds.

Made of cotton candy and magic,
this child holds the secret to all things
beautiful within her sight; a dark night
with the light of the Creator's galaxies
reminds her, that there is no time here;
there is no illusion.

The veil of unknowing does not yet
cover eyes steeped in wonder; heavenly
beings surround and protect this child;
for children are our hope for the future.
They are the ones who will be left
to bring back the magic; to heal
all that has been destroyed; create a new world.

Blessèd be the little ones and their undying
hope and Faith. Life will be reborn
with all the joy and wonder little
children are made of.

Stardust, each one, radiating their aura
of peace upon the cosmic wonder of
this beautiful place we call home.

Daydream

I sat and watched the swans
gliding by. The weeping willow
was sighing low as she whispered
a secret to the waters of life;
silver reflection swept the surface
at her branch tips.
The wildlife here speaking
to one another with Grace, belong
to the energy and life of this place.
The green hues of spring,
the depth of the lake; take a deep,
deep breath.

Draw in the stillness that surrounds you.
You hear the occasional call of the loon;
all too soon, the sun begins to set.

As you lift yourself off the bench,
sweeping eyes across the quiet
stillness of the waters which radiate
magic, you promise yourself
you will return sooner next time,
so the day does not go by too quickly;
the journey through daydreams can linger
a little longer in the heart.

Paper & the Word: A Love Story

An empty page always awaits
the soothing touch of words.

The warmth of human hand
sliding smoothly over page's
skin; hypnotic.

Touch of lead as it speaks
to paper; queries of what happens;
how magic unfolds with word's touch;
a love story which began eons ago.

Paper and word have been
companions since the days of Gilgamesh.

You will find no love greater
than the love of a single sheet of paper
who awaits the powerful and graceful
touch of ~ the Word.

Everything Ends

Everything ends and begins
again in the mortal world.

The day begins and ends, as does
the week, the year; the seasons.

On the flip side; only natural life
and eternal lines of faith.

All that is natural reaches up,
higher than mortal view; tops of trees
we see here on earth, are the same
as those seen by souls who have left;
now on the other side.

Blue sky and glorious sun;
the same blue sky and sun seen
eternally now, in Spirit world.

Mortal meets divine; connected
and more alive.

The difference is: there is no duality,
no darkness in the ethereal: no night,
no clouds, no sorrow ~ only the sweet
and endless sounds of love, light and laughter.

I ...

I view; I see.
I love; I dream.
I will *always* have
faith in human kindness.

I learn; I grow.
I plant; I sew
seeds of compassion
in the deep, moist
soil of my soul's garden.

I hurt; I cry.
I care; I try
to give to others from
my living truth.
I believe in me.
I believe in you.

I will live; I will die.
I will touch; hope to find
the great and sacred reason
for the creative and divine
plan of mortal evolution.

I will stretch; I will reach.
I will laugh, and feel glee
every moment I am able;
mortal soul balanced
and stable in the passionate
search for knowledge and truth.

Cotton Candy Boat

Sitting in a coffee shop
in the heart of the city,
as colours of the sunset
splay out and slowly
fade from the sky.

A multitude of clouds have
absorbed all the picturesque
hues of the setting sun;
lighting up the clouds,
turning the white, billowy
ones into cotton candy
drifting across the evening
above me.

Look up; smile.

Imagine; just imagine
the endless creative possibilities
flowing through the recesses
of your mind; so many
places to travel.

Drift away upon a sea
of divine colour, flowing through the sky.

A cotton candy boat;
you are the captain.
Smooth sailing without a thought
of the world below.

Violet Petals

Violet, mauve, purple ~ all the colours
of highest vibration.

Glorious in their beauty, bringing
to mind fields of lavender and lilac.
Scent permeates my world, like the tender
petals placed upon such loveliness.

I dream in shades of violet hue; shooting
out in all directions; floral feathers
in my view.

Sitting within a cloud, radiating soothing
energy to the world below; such a stunning
display of cosmic vibrance .

Like lace upon a pillow, soothing the soul;
all shades of this spectrum were meant
to be borne for such splendor as this.

Blow me a kiss as I lay my head down
in a garden of violet petals.

A Mother's Hands

A Mother's hands, made of the fine
clay of healing, give freely to heal
the maladies of those they love.

A Mother's hands soothe and comfort
after the bad dreams and worries of little children.

A Mother's hands bring love in every touch,
and as such, she holds the power of creation.

A Mother's hands, pray every day, for
the world.
She nurtures the growth of everything
around her.

A Mother's hands and heart, rarely
consider self: selfless, unconditional
love is the dream for which
she lives.

A Mother's hands hold the magic
of the ages; for only she turns the pages
of her book; her journey through
this thing we call Life.

As Old As I Used to Be

The surrealistic aspect
of change refuses to adjust.

Every single thing about
my life is different; I must
keep telling myself,
you can do this!

I am finding a constant
flux of change, at this older
age, is like being hit regularly
with a battering ram.
Just when I begin to relax
and work on adjusting, BAM ~
something else changes!

Thank goodness I'll not
be this age again; because,
I am not as old as I used to be
ya know.

Through the Veil You Walk
(For my dear, dear brother, Patrick, who walked through the veil December 11, 2020)

Your shamrock is opening
it's beautiful, little white flowers.
I have it by the big window to receive
the sun's light and warmth.

To me, this is a sign from you;
you *will* be okay.

All the souls whom you love,
having now gone, surround you
as they prepare to accompany
you home safely.

My heart sends you love.
My soul sends you remembrance.
My mind will be at peace, when
I know you are, dear brother.

We will miss your kind, warm heart:
your smile: your laughter, your goofy
child within.

Most importantly, we will hold
all your love within us, forever
in our hearts.

I will surely miss you.
I will speak to you often.
I love you with all my heart and soul.

Through the veil you now walk;
comforted, loved and guided
by those you love who have
gone before.

A Million Shining Hearts

Leaves, picked up by the wind,
hit my window; clicking sounds,
as tiny crystals, ring upon the glass.

Gales of November howl through
the atmosphere.

A haunting sound.

Small tornadoes whisk the leaves
and pinecones in the yard.

Outside my front window, tree
branches sway and dance, keeping
rhythm with the wind.

I am lifted with the storm; I fly,
seeking the fae-folk.
Perhaps in the boughs of the large,
powerful oak?

Magic walks here.

Led to a place where all our senses
feel familiarity in everything the eyes
look upon

Pictures of the House of Spirit rose
in my mind; wings move a little faster
until I can hear the welcome sighs
of a million shining hearts.

The Unseen Lands of Here and There

The poet finds words everywhere;
picks them tenderly from the air.
Inspired by an unseen hand, the vessel
moves in accordance with Divine will.

Road signs all around; if you lift your
head, rather than look at the ground.

Sounds of the spheres echo with bliss;
we all know a poet lives and travels
in the unseen lands of here and there.

Walking a fine line, foot in each world,
as a trapeze artist on a tightwire;
delicate balance to maintain.

We live, we breathe, we love with
the word; more powerful than the sharpest
blade, whose appearance comes
with no sound; stealth ~ it's greatest strength.

One word reverberates the world around;
one word we hear through the din ~
open your door so *Love* can come in.

Christmas Eve Musings: 2020

Great Creator, you have wrapped
me in the arms of the Mother;
this poet's place ~ and I sigh.

I give praise to you for a multitude
of small blessings, threaded
tenderly through the fabric
of this life I live:

Laughter of little children,
the great gift of "Grandmother,"
comfort of the four legged babies
of this home.

… too many gifts to count;
surely they could fill a bound
tome of the highest order.

No fodder; simple truth;
for I am created from but a fragment
of you; evolving spirit child, open
to the guidance of divine cosmic hand.

As the music plays at the end of my day,
I merge into a peaceful calm with something
much bigger than I.

I drift upon the shores of peace,
percussion touches inner rhythm
as flute lifts me through the spheres.

I am here ~ now;
in this moment of light and music,
as it soothes mortal sorrows
and brings comfort on this colourful,
yet silent, Christmas Eve.

Crystal Fire

Fold me into a blanket
of crystal fire; purify my soul
with the magic of the ages.

Lay me down in a field
of Hyacinth so I may experience
the rapture of its glorious perfume.

Place me gently upon the surface
of the largest, most dazzling
cloud in the sky; I will look upon
the earth from the heights of Angels.

Carry me down to the ocean;
set me adrift on a sea of peace,
that I may ebb and flow for eternity
upon love's shore.

Clay of the Earth

In the heart of the sun lie
mysteries we may never know.

We are each given seeds to sew,
good and bad; every individual
has a choice.

As leaves blowing in the wind:
we sway, we dance, we fall, we die.

Re-absorbed into clay of the earth;
restful mirth spreads through your
being as you gaze into the cosmic
reality of which *you* are an integral part.

A Million Stars

I am a child of the cosmos.
I have wings that I may fly.

I wear the white robes
of innocence: long, cascading
ribbons of empathy and compassion
walk with me.

As I step through the portal
between worlds, I can hear
the crackle of spiritual spark.

There is no dark here; all is
illuminated under the heavens.

Rainbow shines above me,
as the promise of eternity rests
deep in my mortal bones.

When I return home, the light
of a million stars shall guide me.

This Great Lady

Put your ear to the ground;
you can hear the sound
of the earth breathing.

Listen to a tree as you bend
on your knee to hear rivers
of life running from root to crown.

Sit down in the shade of a tall,
blue spruce, she will embrace you
and keep you cool through the hot
days of summer.

Walk along forest trails, feet sure
upon the ground; foot sounds
will echo among the elders of this
natural place; they have a face.
Each one, as we, has its own personality.

Touch the waters of this land as you
stand in prayer, your arms lifted
unto heaven in reverence for the majesty
of this great lady.

Essence

Naught but sorrow flows
through my veins; deep
heartache pushes rivers
of love to my eyes; rivulets
run salty and warm down
my cheeks.

Grief is a roiling ocean of emotion
running through the flower fields
within you.

I learned long ago, there can
be great, yet bittersweet beauty
in suffering.

I have also learned, the poet views
through the senses and lenses
of a different sight.

Suffering cleanses mortal soul
and brings us closer to the divine
within self.

We must believe in the grace
and mercy of divine love.

When the Creator calls us home,
we *must* listen.
For this is a new chapter in
the evolution of one human soul.

Moondust

The moon in all its radiance
shines golden through your hair.
A world of dancing moonbeams
shining 'round you, glistening fair.

Stars glow bright in your heaven;
moondrops glisten and dance in your eyes.
I can see there's shimmering silver within
the beautiful blue of your skies.

I see in the aura around you,
your healing is part of the plan;
you hold so much to give others;
a kind and soft-hearted man.

You need to learn to forgive yourself;
how to love yourself once again.
You have been awakened from your sleep;
no longer can you pretend.

Dry your tears, love; look to your dreams,
even though it seem they've all gone.
These dreams will find their way back to you
when you can hear your own spirit song.

Close your eyes and say a prayer
with all the passion you feel evermore;
love in all her radiant light
stands knocking upon your door.

Step for Step

In a crowd, or in a darkened room;
on a street, under light of lady moon,
you stand before me.

I cannot be alone here, so deeply
entranced in love's magic.

Each time we touch, the ache grows.

How do I tell you, in a world of impressions,
I recognize you; I know you, and how I sigh
when you touch me with the love you bring.

I cannot touch on my canvas of words
what I see in you: pure, total, complete.
You light every candle in this room;
you seem to know the words to every
tune my heart sings.

You know every step of the dance
of my spirit.

A chorus of angels surrounds us, bringing
us, step for step, ever closer to the dream
we are destined to share.

Within the Crystal

I think about you often, friend;
I wonder how you do?
Is there someone with you caring?
Is there someone loving you?

Do you walk through the land of shadows?
Does the sun shine through on you?
Reach out, my friend, and ask me ~
is there something I can do?

Hope seems to have faded;
each day, another trial.
So hard, so hard to find much joy;
so hard these days to smile.

Listen; hear the sun arise.
Each day a prayer shines anew.
You've got the strength, you've got the will;
courage lives in you.

I'll be there through your painful times
should you need a hand to hold.
I'll help you find your peace again
as you learn to heal your soul.

There truly are bright days ahead.
There's hope, good fortune too.
All you need to do, dear friend,
is look inside of you.

Language of Music

Music ripples through me
like raindrops at pond's edge.
Passionate movement begins, rising
up from the core of my being.
Watch me dance ~ I will sing along
with the melodies, matching
them with this heart.
As beat strengthens, so does
passion rise, as the flames
of eternal bliss.
Leave me this, alone in this reverie
of tunes played by cosmic fingers,
orchestrated by the angels over us.
We think we know bliss; perhaps
we do, a concept best understood
within the limits and confines
of our mortal minds.
As tone rises, so spirit rises
to the enchanting levels of other
dimensions, other realities.
So *much* is possible through
this language of music.
All spirits know this language
of the spheres, surrounding
and permeating our being.
We are seeing through spirit eye,
with central focus on Paradise,
where universal spheres play all around
and within; laid out before us as a true
promise from the Creator, in the forgiveness
of our humanity.

Wings Upon Angels

I am a ray of light, shining from the heavens,
leaving itself within this corporeal vessel.
I am a star which has been mortalized from
the dust of universal truth.
I am the sky on a clear day; the moon,
reflecting through night's darkness.
I am mortal; I am soft.
I am compassion enfolded in the dreams
of angels.
I am the teardrop which forms from
the sorrow of a broken heart.
I am the wind, blowing its comfort,
the sea upon which mortal heals.

I am the sun that warms; giver of life
in a brilliant world.
I am the torment found in the depths
of mortal despair: the abyss, the darkness
beneath our earthly feet.
I am the world, struggling to reach
the light of all truth.
I am the peace, so elusive, in this world of pain.
I am the seeker, looking for wisdom
to overcome and rise up from the ruin
of emotional struggle, trying hard to juggle,
to get to know the various parts of self.

I am the elf of ancient folklore; the one
we see no more. We have lost the magic.
I am a magnet learning to manifest
all those things I desire, whilst learning
to transcend higher into soul, slowly
becoming whole once again.

I am the faerie in the tall meadow grass,
looking for something we lack.
I am the wings upon angels.

I am nothing. I am everything. I am.

Kindred to the Magpie

I am kindred to the Magpie,
for I too am a lover of all things
which shine and sparkle.
I sing my song within; Magpie
sings his song without.
I am kindred to the Magpie.

I have wings to fly the same as he;
in a different place in a human like me.
My heart has found its wings.
I can fly, I am free.
I am kindred to the Magpie.

Unique is the call of this shadowy bird;
he can also learn to speak
human words; a dark silhouette
who flies with the crow and the raven.
I am kindred to the Magpie.

He is the thief who will steal
the stars from the sky, the bright
dust of the universe, to hide in
the depths of his nest, so he may look
upon them often, bedazzled by
the shiny glow.
I am kindred to the Magpie.

He dreams in stardust; he flies among
sky's clouds: ever proud, every whole;
a wild and wingèd soul is he.
Magpie can be tamed to cohabit with mortals;
it is here they are able to learn
our language.

Wonder ~ do they understand the Word?
I am kindred to this bird.

White Lion
(First African serial rights donated to whitelions.org
for their promotion and repopulation of the white
lions in the wild. In 2015, they were close to releasing the first
of them)

White lion of majesty, strength and grace,
show me the infinite world in which you live.
One with Mother Earth; upon your birth
the forest bowed in reverence to your great spirit.

White lion of the forest: of desert and the plain,
teach me about loyalty, power and courage.
As you bow low in admiration for the mother,
your mind touches the earth and replenishes
your strength.

White lion, with your mane surrounding
the beauty of your face; eyes look upon forest floor.
I can see memories of loss within your mind;
the instinct to move on, walk on, fight on.

White lion of great beauty, touch the heart
within me; share the secret of the truth
you live as you roam.

White lion, King of all felines, you possess
and aura of wisdom hidden in the fierce
heart of your powerful soul.

Star Traveller

I step through the portal.
The veil has been lifted.
I am surrounded by the crystal
magnificence of sight: clear,
fresh, alive.
I see all dimensions through
this view; gateway to multiple
universes of radiance.
Awe surrounds me: wonder
elevates me, peace layers other
worlds before me as I place
my foot upon solid ground.
The crackle of a forest floor
moves beneath my feet; it echoes
and reverberates through the sweet
scent of love. I have risen above
the vanities and ego of the world
I left behind.

It is a new beginning, as portals open
before me, one after another; I may
choose the path I walk.

I am a star traveler;
a multitude of choices I could
make; yet only one my soul
would desire; the one with all
the magic a heart could hold.

A Brighter Day

Through the realm of Spirit
heart beats strong;
aflame with passion, we move
constantly between dimensions.
Shifting variance creates
soulful rhythm.

Within the whole, well-being
thrives: soma overflows
eternal cup, Angels sing
in unison with cosmic tide.
Upon their wings, I ride the ether.

Sing to me, sweet Angels,
a lullaby from my home.
Comfort my heart with
the Love and Mercy
of cosmic being.

The sight I am seeing,
of soft cloud sky
passes by my open
consciousness into
the recesses of time.

Love shall shine and lead
the way to a brand new
world and a brighter day.

A Kelly Warrior

My mind was once so sharp, so strong;
it's hard to accept this lifetime thing,
all because I carry a bum gene.
Hereditary, they are not sure -
I am - for my dad suffered as I do.

It strikes without warning; like a thief
sneaking up behind you.
Now, after this week past, I realize there
is no part of me it has left alone.
My eyes, now starting, hopefully
it will not morph into the nightmares
I have heard of by others with Behcet's.

Recent new symptoms of neurological
impairment; frustration, confusion -
don't know that I will ever "get used"
to it all - with illness, unfortunately,
it does not always work that way.
Many have been given life sentences;
their bodies have betrayed the good
mind and passionate heart; the heart
that just wants to "be free" to *do*.
In this case, depression is, unfortunately,
one of the genetic components of
Behcet's Disease.

I am fortunate, when it hits, it does not
generally last for more than a week or so.
I have developed self-help, coping activities
which generally get me through - and out the
other side I fly - filled with sunshine once again.

Yes, it gets me down - yes, it frustrates me,
yes, I miss the whiz bang I used to be
when it came to business.
As we grow older in our years, all of us
encounter different challenges and difficulties;
we hold different dreams, plan different goals
and through it all we hold, hold, hold on.

This is not a writing of victim stance.
It is a writing about courage to face the unknown.
Strength to get through your body's brutal
assault upon you on a day to day basis.
It is about never losing your ability for smiling,
'nor your sense of humour for too long.
It will take vacations from time to time;
and if it is away too long – don't go looking for it;
enjoy the freedom, it will return soon enough.

I will come through this too, as I always do.
Though I find that with each new symptom
I experience, I also experience a mixture of sadness
with a little fear.

I will come through this, as I always do.
That's just what Kelly Warrior's do.

A Note To Behçet's

Behçet's is causing me problems,
they are tough ones I don't like.
I wish that it would listen to me
when I tell it to *take a hike!*

In anticipation of major surgery,
my anxiety is taking its toll.
Behçet's is acting terribly,
a bully of body and soul.

It's hard to keep my Spirits up;
more difficult each and every day.
I do not know what it has in store,
don't worry, my heart seems to say.

Be at peace, just know you are safe,
in the care of Creator's loving say.
In the face of this bully I *will* be strong
and tell Behçet's to be on its way

So, when the day is before me
I will call on Guardians and healers Divine,
to be sure everything runs smoothly
and I walk away doing fine.

I give my thanks, every day,
an Angel has come to my aid.
He's taken mortal burden from me
and offered my debt to be paid.

This Angel is part of our family,
a kind heart of thoughtful deeds.
I thank you, Lord, for giving
this wonderful brother to me.

So you see, Behçet's, I'm supported,
making it a little easier to kick your ass;
You must know I am stronger than you are,
and your influence, weakened will pass.

Once again I will be the warrior,
the one who came to throw you out.
I will, yet again, be the victor,
of this, I have nary a doubt!

A Pittance from Few

My heart for a nickel
the beggar said,
just enough to get home;
to buy me some bread.

My heart for a penny
the little child said,
just enough for some candy;
a pillow for my head.

My heart for a nickel
the old woman said,
just enough to get better;
buy some medicine, doc said.

My heart for a penny
the sad one said,
just one to toss in a wishing well;
wish for happiness instead.

My heart for a nickel
the grandmother said,
just enough for a memory of
your father, long dead.

My heart for a penny
the older brother said,
just enough to let me help
those who have no bed.

My heart for a nickel
the sad woman said,
just enough to trigger memory;
the lights of stardom shone in red.

When all the nickels and all of the pennies
are gathered from around the globe,
trumpets sound, love resounds -
and sharing begins to unfold.

Akashic Connection

The Akashic connection
is carried within us.
We *all* hold the knowledge
of the cosmos; remember,
stardust, of which we are made,
is an eternal substance;
existing long before *any*
life began. This knowledge breaks
through in sight and sound.

The complexities of
cosmic events could *not ever*
be grasped completely
with conscious, mortal mind.

Journey to your inner
eternal being; there, within
grasp, a light shines
strong and bright, filled
to overflowing with
the great fire of complete,
eternal knowledge; yours
to hold close to your heart.

*(In theosophy and anthroposophy, the **Akashic records** are a compendium of all human events, thoughts, words, emotions, and intent ever to have occurred in the past, present, or future. They are believed by theosophists to be encoded in a non-physical plane of existence known as the etheric plane).*

The Hippie

A vestige of the Hippie will
always remain in me.
Faith found in a universal sharing
of Love and of peace.
We looked at what was
and had the courage to
believe in what *could* be;
anything was possible within
the eternal and spiritual dream
of our society.
The ageless and memorable
revolution of this place has
been sold out by most
to the nameless and shadowed
corporate face;
sold out to be able to share
in the deceit and cold selfishness
of the corporate machine.
And why would they agree
with the concept of Love and peace?
There is far more profit
in war and disease.
Left in a time of nowhere,
unable to even remember
the free, unfettered spirit who
once believed in you and me,
the one who once vowed never, ever
to do what we had been told *must* be...
and to hold on strong -
to the spirit of, *"The Hippie."*

Biography

Deborah L. Kelly lives in Prince George, *B.C.,* and has had her works published in numerous anthologies, books, and literary magazines, both in Canada and Internationally. Prior to relocating in Northern B.C., *Deborah* hosted at *Poetic Justice, and Poetry in the Park* in New Westminster, throughout the year. *Deborah* has also been a featured presenter at *Poetry in the Park, Holy Wow Poets, Surrey Muse, World Poetry, Edge of the Page Poetry, and The Tagore Society.*
Deborah has also co-hosted and appeared on a number of occasions on *World Poetry Co-Op Radio* in Vancouver. *Deborah's* debut poetry collection, *Through My Eyes*, was published in 2015 by Silver Bow Publishing. She also placed an impressive Fourth in the Rabindranath Tagore Awards, 2015, for her work, *Voices of Nature*, and received Honorable Mention in 2016, for her work, *Gems of Humanity.* For her short story, *I Am Jin, Deborah* placed second and was awarded India's Bharat Award, 2017, Distinguished Writer International, 2017. *Deborah* served as Director/Secretary with

New Westminster's *Royal City Literary Arts Society, 2013/14,* and hosted all society workshops. In May 2016, *Deborah* was the recipient of the Dr. Asha Bhargava Memorial, *"Distinguished Poet Award,"* from Writers International Network (WIN-Canada).

Deborah's second book, *Spirit'Song,* was published by XpressPublications.com in association with the *Rabindranath Tagore Society and Poiesis International*, India, 2016. Her third book, *Heartworks,* Silver Bow Publishing, 2016. *Cry of Humanity, Deborah's* fourth book, was launched by Silver Bow Publishing in June 2018; *Songs of the North*, published by Ekstatis Editions, 2020, and is now working on her next book, *Darkness Shadows Light.*

Deborah is now retired, and is enjoying the Northern life, on the edge of the midnight sun, where she spends her days gardening, enjoying her grandchildren and writing poetry.

E-mail: poetrybydeborah@gmail.com

www.ingramcontent.com/pod-product-compliance
Lightning Source LLC
Chambersburg PA
CBHW021433070526
44577CB00001B/182